Jaime J. Sucher

Golden Retrievers

Second Edition

Everything about Purchase, Care, Nutrition, Diseases, Behavior, and Breeding

With 40 Color Photographs;
45 Illustrations by Michele Earle-Bridges

Consulting Editor: Matthew M. Vriends, Ph.D.

BARRON'S

All inquiries should be addressed to:
Barron's Educational Series, Inc.
250 Wireless Boulevard
Hauppauge, NY 11788

International Standard Book No. 0-8120-9019-5

Library of Congress Catalog Card No. 94-44864

**Library of Congress Cataloging-in-Publication
Data**

Sucher, Jaime J.
    Golden retrievers : everything about purchase,
care, nutrition, breeding, behavior, and training /
Jaime J. Sucher; illustrations by Michele Earle-
Bridges; consulting editor, Matthew M. Vriends.—
2nd ed.
        p. cm.
    Includes index.
    ISBN 0-8120-9019-5
    1. Golden retrievers. I. Title.
SF429.G63S83 1995   94-44864
636.7′52—dc20   CIP

Printed in Hong Kong

678   9955   987

About the Author

Jaime Sucher is an animal nutritionist who has written on a wide variety of canine topics. Among his
books for Barron's are *Shetland Sheepdogs* and
Shih Tzu.

Photo Credits

Barbara Augello: page 9, inside back cover;
Eugene Butenas (LCA Photography): 17, 36,
77, 84; Susan Green: inside front cover, pages
4, 16, 21, 29, 33, 37, (bottom right); D.J. Hamer:
37 (top), 60; Raymond D. Kopen 25, 37 (bottom
left); Judith Strom: 12, 13, 24, 28, 32, 45, 49,
52, 61, 64 (bottom), 72, 73, 76, 81, back cover;
Wim Van Vught: front cover, 8, 57, 64 (top), 85.

Important Note

This pet owner's guide tells the reader how
to buy and care for a golden retriever. The
author and the publisher consider it important
to point out that the advice given in the book is
meant primarily for normally developed puppies from a good breeder—that is, dogs of
excellent physical health and good character.
    Anyone who adopts a fully grown dog should
be aware that the animal has already formed its
basic impressions of human beings. The new
owner should watch the animal carefully,
including its behavior toward humans, and
should meet the previous owner. If the dog
comes from a shelter, it may be possible to get
some information on the dog's background and
peculiarities there. There are dogs that as a
result of bad experiences with humans behave
in an unnatural manner or may even bite. Only
people that have experience with dogs should
take in such an animal.
    Caution is further advised in the association
of children with dogs, in meetings with other
dogs, and in exercising the dog without a leash.
    Even well-behaved and carefully supervised
dogs sometimes do damage to someone
else's property or cause accidents. It is therefore in the owner's interest to be adequately
insured against such eventualities, and we
strongly urge all dog owners to purchase a lia-
bility policy that covers their dog.

Preface

When Sir Dudley Marjoriebanks, the first Lord Tweedmouth, developed the golden retriever, he could not have foreseen the breed becoming as popular as it is today. To dog authorities, however, the reason for this popularity is obvious.

The golden is one of the greatest of all hunting dogs. It has the scenting power of the bloodhound, as well as all of the abilities of a setter and a retriever. This breed is extremely successful on land, but its greatest ability is in retrieving from water. The golden has a soft mouth, and it is able to withstand the temperatures of the coldest ponds and streams. It is hardy, proud, tough, and shows great endurance—all of which makes it an ideal companion for the sportsman.

Like most hunting dogs, goldens are easy to train. They are eager learners, extremely obedient, and very patient. These factors have made the golden retriever very popular among sportsmen and a dominant breed in both the field and the obedience ring.

Although originally bred for hunting, the golden, through generations of careful breeding and the influence of the close human-canine relationship, has developed a unique temperament. Few breeds can match the golden's friendly, loving, and gentle nature; fewer still display its innate love for children. In addition, goldens are naturally clean, easy to groom, and suffer from few genetic diseases. All of these qualities make the golden retriever an ideal family pet.

Unfortunately, in recent years it has been shown that these traits cannot be taken for granted. The increase in the golden's popularity has led to careless breeding practices by people whose primary concern is for profits. As a result of these practices, an increasing number of goldens suffer from physical and behavioral problems.

This practical manual will tell you everything you need to know about choosing and raising a golden retriever. It will answer your questions about keeping a dog in your house or in a kennel. Detailed instructions tell you how to help the dog adapt to its new home and how to feed and care for it. This manual also provides information about preventive medicine, symptoms of illness, and treatment of various injuries and diseases.

A chapter traces the breed's origin and history, describes the basic behavioral patterns of goldens, as well as of dogs in general, and outlines the breed standard. There is also a chapter devoted entirely to training your golden retriever. For novice dog owners, it provides the fundamentals of instruction needed to develop a sound program for daily practice sessions. It is also hoped that experienced owners may find new ideas to incorporate into their daily regimen.

I would like to acknowledge the assistance of Matthew Vriends, Ph.D., consulting editor of this series, Helgard Niewisch, D.V.M, who reviewed the manuscript, and Fredric L. Frye, D.V.M., whose many suggestions are incorporated in this new edition.

Jaime J. Sucher
Spring, 1995

Should You Buy a Golden Retriever?

Making an Intelligent Choice

Golden retrievers have quickly become one of the most popular purebreed dogs in America. Although originally bred for hunting, goldens have shown tremendous versatility, and they excel in other areas as well. They have been used by authorities in searching out explosives and narcotics, and have proven to be reliable Seeing-Eye dogs. However, in recent years, goldens have made their greatest impact as family pets.

The popularity of the golden retriever, to an extent, is very much a reflection of our modern society's concept of the perfect family dog. It is a very attractive breed that requires a minimum of grooming to keep it in "show" condition. Goldens are reasonably clean, and they are very easy to maintain in top physical and mental health. They also possess the ideal temperament for a family dog.

Goldens are "people" dogs. They are a friendly, gentle, and eager breed that truly need human companionship. Anyone who takes the time and effort to establish a positive rapport with a golden will be rewarded with a loving and affectionate friend that will do anything to please his or her master.

Goldens are easy to train because they really love to learn. Their favorite time may well be the training session. This breed has the ability to learn practically anything a human can teach a dog to do. This trait has made them a popular hunting dog as well as a dominant force in the obedience ring.

Although these qualities may be found in all goldens, the owner must be sure they are developed and become part of the dog's personality. Bringing out the best in your dog will take time, energy, patience, and understanding.

An Adult or a Puppy?

One of the great rewards of owning a golden retriever is watching it grow from an awkward, tiny bundle of fur into a thoroughly trained, well-behaved, beautiful adult. However, this requires a great deal of patience, time, and energy. If you work diligently with your puppy during the early training phases, you will be rewarded with the most loving four-legged companion imaginable. However, if your puppy is given little training, it may grow up to be eighty pounds of unruly hyperactivity—a situation that no dog owner could cope with for very long.

Therefore, selecting an adult golden also offers advantages. A well-trained adult makes a marvelous pet. It can save you the time and effort needed for rearing and training a puppy. Mature goldens almost always adapt easily to new owners and environments. A housebroken, trained adult golden makes an ideal companion for owners for whom raising puppies may be too much work. The greatest drawback to buying an older golden is that you may find it extremely difficult to correct any bad habits the dog has already acquired.

When choosing between a golden puppy and an adult, keep in mind that raising a puppy will allow you to train it to the habits of your home. Adult dogs, on the other hand, need significantly less attention, which means less work and effort, especially for an older owner.

Important Note: To buy, or not to buy, a golden retriever is an important decision. Many people who purchase dogs are not aware of all the responsibilities of dog ownership at the time of purchase. This lack of awareness usually results in an unhappy relationship for both dog and owner. Therefore, before you buy a golden retriever, carefully consider the following points:

• First and foremost, are you looking for a watchdog? If the answer is "yes," then the golden retriever is not for you. As stated earlier, the golden retriever is renowned for its gentleness, an undesirable trait in a watchdog. A golden retriever may bark at a stranger at the door, but its tail will be wagging as an invitation to play.

• Do you have the time, energy, and patience required to raise a dog properly? If you purchase a golden puppy, would you be willing and able to adjust your schedule to meet the dog's needs?

• Are you willing to devote some of your free time to the dog? Do you travel on weekends or take long vacations? Are you willing to travel only to areas where you can bring your golden retriever? Remember that although dogs can withstand the stress of travel fairly well, they are prohibited in many hotels and motels.

• Do you understand the long-term commitment involved in owning a golden retriever? A dog should never be purchased impulsively, especially because a golden may live a dozen years or more.

• Do you have a large yard, or is there a park or woods nearby where your dog can get its much needed exercise? A golden is a remarkable breed and can adapt to any living quarters that can sensibly house a medium-large breed. However, because the golden is bred for hunting, exercise is an important part of its physical and mental well-being.

• Finally, can you afford to keep a golden retriever? Aside from the initial expenses of buying the dog and purchasing necessary supplies, the cost of feeding may go as high as $40 per month. And don't forget additional expenses such as annual visits to the veterinarian.

You should consider these questions carefully before you buy a golden retriever. Find out if there is a chapter of the Golden Retriever Club of America in your area. This organization can help answer any questions you may have. Remember, owning a dog of any breed is a serious responsibility. If you do not care for the dog properly, its health and happiness will suffer, and you will not experience the pleasure and satisfaction of raising a golden retriever.

If you are looking for a show dog, you have two options. First, you can purchase a potential show puppy from a reputable breeder and raise it yourself. This way you will have the satisfaction of knowing that you have done the job yourself. If you do not need this satisfaction, you can purchase a mature show dog; this way you are assured of your golden's quality and beauty.

Whether you choose a puppy or an adult is an extremely important decision. However, the choice of the sex of the dog is not always as important. Golden females (bitches) are just as good a choice as males. Females are usually only slightly smaller and lighter than males. In addition, there is no significant difference in temperament between the sexes.

These adorable puppies are typical of what you will see when searching for your new dog. Be sure that the dog you choose possesses a golden's temperament as well as it's looks.

The only time you might prefer a specific sex is if you are interested in breeding the dog. If you are considering starting a kennel, females are preferable. If you select a female and have no intention of breeding her, have the dog neutered. Because there are an alarming number of homeless dogs in the United States, owners should take all possible precautions against the needless proliferation of unwanted animals. Another advantage of neutering is avoiding the messiness that will occur when she is "in heat." The female will also be more likely to avoid breast tumors, ovarian cysts, false pregnancies, and other ailments if she has been neutered.

Note that if you plan to enter your female in a dog show, she will be disqualified if she is neutered. A neutered dog, however, may compete in field and obedience trials.

Selecting the Right Puppy for You

While visiting all the reputable dealers and breeders on your list, pay special attention to the following factors. Above all, a golden must be healthy and possess a temperament typical of the breed. When you first look at a puppy, you will see only an adorable energetic bundle of fur and wrinkles. Learn to see past this, and resist the impulse to buy the first puppy that catches your fancy. Examine the puppy's coat; it should be smooth and shiny. Its eyes should be bright and have a friendly and curious expression. It should be solidly built. Remember also that goldens are very people-oriented, and this should be obvious even at an early age. Look for an eager, alert puppy with a wagging tail, and avoid both hyperactive and overly sedate dogs.

Another good indicator of the puppy's temperament is its mother's behavior. After all, many of the puppy's behavioral characteristics are inherited from its sire (father) or dam (mother). Observe how the mother reacts to people. She should be friendly and show no signs of fear or apprehension.

If the puppy appears to be in good health and of sound temperament, the next step is to check its pedigree papers. These papers are a written record of the dog's recent ancestry. Like most medium and large breeds, some bloodlines of goldens suffer from hip dysplasia. Many breeders will have their dogs examined for this disease by the Orthopedic Foundation for Animals (OFA). Dogs that are free of this ailment are given an OFA number that is placed on the pedigree. In addition, numbers are given to dogs that have had their eyes checked and cleared. Never purchase a dog whose pedigree papers lack these numbers.

If the dog's pedigree is satisfactory, ask for the date the puppy was wormed, and be sure to get a written record of this for later use by your veterinarian. Do not be afraid to ask questions. Reputable dealers and breeders are just as concerned with the puppy's welfare as you are.

Do not be offended if a breeder asks questions about your experience with dogs and where you plan to raise your puppy. Take this as a sign of concern. In addition, keep an open line of communication with the breeder so that he or she can help you with any future problems.

Take plenty of time when making your final choice. As previously mentioned, at first all puppies will look cute and very much alike. Watch them carefully, however, and their subtle differences will become more apparent. By watching them play together, you can get a better idea of their individual temperaments. Some may be bolder,

Golden puppies are outgoing, friendly, and find pleasure in just about everything they do. Avoid all dogs that are quick to show signs of fear.

others shyer; the puppy's temperament is the best indicator of its adult behavior. Again, do not hesitate to ask for help.

Where and How to Buy a Golden Retriever

The first thing to do when searching for a good quality golden retriever is to visit the dealers and the golden kennels in your area. The secretary of the Golden Retriever Club of America, your local Golden Club, or the American Kennel Club can all help you obtain a list of reputable dealers and breeders in your area. Make appointments to inspect the dogs and the conditions in which they are kept. It is best to make as many visits as possible, regardless of the distance involved, since it is important to get a healthy, well-cared-for dog. The time you spend finding the right dog will save you a great deal of effort and heartbreak later on.

Remember that the quality of your puppy will be a direct reflection of the quality of the breeder. Conscientious dealers obtain puppies from conscientious breeders who will make every effort to maintain their reputation.

You should never be tempted to buy a "cheap" dog. The old adage, "You get what you pay for," is all too true in purchasing a dog. A lower priced dog may mean it was raised strictly for profit by an inexperienced breeder, or that it is in poor health. You should also avoid purchasing a puppy from a kennel that is not dedicated solely to raising golden retrievers. Breeders who raise several breeds are not always knowledgeable about the special needs of each breed.

Once you have selected the puppy that is best for you, you will have to arrange to take it home. The puppy should be seven weeks old when it moves into its new home. A puppy of this age should adapt very easily to its new environment, yet it should not be old enough to have picked up many bad habits. Recent studies have shown that during their eighth week, puppies become especially sensitive to environmental changes. If you cannot pick up the puppy during the seventh week, wait until the ninth week. Rather than risk behavioral problems, wait until the puppy is ready for change.

How Much Will It Cost?

The initial purchase price of a golden retriever varies; however, expect to spend at least $200. Puppies from champion caliber parents may sell for as much as $1000 or more. A younger puppy will usually be less expensive that an older dog, because less time and money will have been invested in it. The closer an older puppy is to being a show dog, the more expensive it will be. Remember that the extra money you spend initially may save you a great deal of money on veterinary bills, as well as the heartache that accompanies a poorly reared dog. Licensing fees also vary greatly, so check with your local town hall or animal shelter.

As stated earlier, food may cost as much as $40 a month, and you must also purchase certain equipment for feeding, grooming, and housing your dog. Veterinary fees must also be considered. A dog requires annual immunizations against all infectious diseases, as well as an annual heartworm test. A puppy may also have to be wormed. If your dog should get sick or injured, it may need additional, costly medical attention.

Finally, you will have to pay a fee to register your dog with the American Kennel Club, as well as annual dues if you join the Golden Retriever Club of America.

You can see that the expenses of owning a golden retriever are much greater than the initial purchase price. Therefore, carefully consider these costs before you buy a dog.

Housing and Supplies

Indoor Space Requirements

A golden retriever, whether a puppy or an adult, needs a reasonably spacious, quiet living area where it can feel comfortable and secure. Inside your home you must provide the dog with a "territory" of its own. This territory will represent your dog's feeding and sleeping areas. In order for your dog to feel protected, these areas should not be moved. A dog will only feel secure if it has a quiet, reliable place to rest undisturbed. This area should neither isolate the dog nor should it be subject to heavy human traffic.

Good resting areas are most often found in corners where the dog is protected on two sides. These areas should also be draft-free and not in direct sunlight. The dog's sleeping area should also make it easy to confine its movements when you go to bed or when you leave the house.

Whelping box and sleeping baskets. Make certain that the one you make or choose is large enough for a full-grown golden to lie down in comfortably.

Several types of dog carriers are available. Small carriers with a single handle (top left) are suitable for golden puppies. An adult golden would require a larger carrier, such as the wire cage on a platform (lower right).

Your choice of a sleeping box and pad, or a cage with pad, will depend on your method of housebreaking. (See the chapter entitled, "Basic and Advanced Training"). I recommend using a cage, as it can also be invaluable for transporting and disciplining your puppy. Dogs are instinctively den animals, and the confined space of a cage will make a puppy feel safer and more comfortable than an open sleeping box.

The cage should be approximately 24 inches (61 cm) high, by 24 inches (61 cm) wide, by 36 inches (91 cm) long. The construction of the cage is important, for it must have strong welds that cannot be broken by a large, active puppy.

The cage will be your puppy's "house" when you are not around to

A well-designed and comfortable dog house offers your golden a place of shelter when it goes outdoors.

supervise it. Some cages can also be used to carry your puppy when you go for a drive or to the veterinarian.

If you decide not to use a cage, purchase a sleeping box. Make sure it is large enough to accommodate a full-grown, spread-out dog. Line the box with cedar shavings and shredded newspapers and then place an old blanket over it. Your dog will find this very comfortable for sleeping. If you decide to build your own box, use only nonsplintering hardwoods. Because many stains and paints are toxic to puppies, leave the box unfinished.

My Tip: Like its sleeping place, a dog's feeding place should never be changed. Changes in sleeping and feeding places can cause your pet unnecessary stress. An animal under stress may exhibit behavioral changes as well as changes in many biological functions, including problems with digestion and excretion. Place your dog's feeding areas in an easily cleaned room such as the kitchen.

Keeping Your Golden Outdoors

When you are not home, your golden will be just as happy (if not happier) outdoors as inside your home. Because a golden retriever is family-oriented, do not keep your dog outdoors for very long periods when you are home. If you are outside working, by all means, bring your dog with you. During these outdoor periods your golden will get its daily exercise.

If you leave your dog outside when you are not home, provide it with a fenced enclosure or run. The run should be at least 6 feet (2 m) wide, by 15 feet (5 m) long, by 6 feet (2 m) high, and it should be constructed of strong chain link fence. You can place partially buried boards around the bottom to prevent the dog from digging under the fence. The run can be as large as your yard. However, it must not be smaller than the size stated.

Use a few inches of smooth stone as a base. This will provide drainage when it rains, and it will prevent the dog from becoming muddy. Do not use concrete as a floor because concrete will retain the smell of urine.

The doghouse. Hinging the roof panels facilitates cleaning and airing.

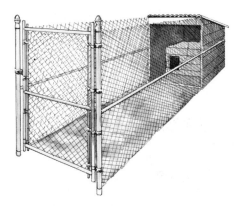

This type of run, complete with shelter, provides your dog with a place to exercise as well as protection from rain, snow, wind, and direct sunlight.

The run must also provide your dog with some shade and shelter.

The best form of outdoor shelter is a doghouse. Whether you build your own or buy one, make sure it is raised several inches off the ground to avoid dampness and insects. The doghouse must be properly constructed to protect the dog against wind, rain, and cold, for even a minor draft can lead to serious respiratory ailments. The doghouse should be approximately 48 inches (122 cm) long, 36 inches (91 cm) high, and 36 inches (91 cm) wide. If the house is too small, the dog will not be able to stand or sleep comfortably. Also, be sure not to make the house overly large because during cold weather the dog's body will provide the only form of heat. For this reason, it is also best to insulate the structure.

You can take several precautions in order to keep the house clean. Place a hinged roof on the house for better access. Line the floor with an easy-to-clean material, such as linoleum, above the flooring so that you can spread cedar shavings and cover them with a blanket.

Finally, make sure that the opening of the house faces south and is not subject to the cold north winds of winter. You can also hang a piece of canvas or blanket over the opening, making sure it overlaps sufficiently to eliminate drafts. If you live in a climate where winter nights can be very cold, I recommend that you find an indoor place where the dog can sleep—unless you have carefully tested the insulation of the doghouse.

Additional Equipment and Accessories

Your puppy's first day at home can be very busy and hectic. To avoid additional work and confusion, purchase the following items and keep them available.

The most important pieces of equipment, at least from your dog's point of view, are its food and water dishes. They should be nonbreakable and heavy, as well as sturdy enough so that a golden with a voracious appetite cannot tip them over. Bowls are available in plastic, stainless steel, and ceramic. If you choose a ceramic bowl, make sure it was not fired with a lead-based glaze.

You may have to purchase more than one collar for your dog as it matures. A puppy needs a light collar but not necessarily a strong one. A small puppy requires only a leather or nylon collar, but bear in mind that these tend to deteriorate with time. In addition, your puppy's neck size will increase considerably as it grows, and not all collars adjust sufficiently. Chain collars are strong enough for an adult golden. I recommend buying your puppy an inexpensive leather or nylon collar and changing to a good chain collar when the dog is nearly full grown. I also recommend purchasing reflecting tags or tape for your dog's collar and leash. These make it easier for a driver to see both dog and master when headlights shine on them, thus making nighttime walks much

Several types of food and water dishes are available. All are sturdy; some include food and water dishes in the same stand.

safer. You should also attach an identity tag with your address and phone number to the dog's collar. This could prove invaluable if your dog ever becomes lost.

Leashes come in a wide variety of lengths and materials, and you may want to purchase more than one type. For regular walks, use a leash only a few feet long. This will enable you to quickly bring the dog to your side if

An identification tag should be attached to your golden's collar.

Collars come in all shapes and sizes and can be made of chain (above), leather, or nylon (below). Collars with slip rings (above) are excellent for training a golden.

Equipment for your golden need not be elaborate or expensive, but it should be carefully selected.

With the proper equipment, the routine grooming your golden requires will become a quick and easy process, and the results will be something you can be proud of.

The beach is a great place to take goldens, as it gives them a lot of space to get their exercise.

This piece of driftwood quickly becomes a retriever's dream toy—a fetching stick.

While some breeds of dog may be bold enough to play fetch at the waters edge...

...the fearless, water-loving golden shows no hesitation as it plunges into the waves to retrieve the stick for its master.

The long or reel leash enables you to adjust the free play when walking your golden.

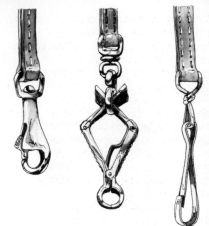

Leashes can attach to collars using a safety catch (left), scissor clip (center), or regular spring clip (right).

you need to. It will also keep the dog from straying too far. If you have sufficient yard space, a 30-foot (9-m) leash with an automatic reel is useful. Remember that golden puppies will chew—or attempt to chew—anything near their mouths. Therefore, you should not purchase a chain leash for a puppy. Chewing on the chain may damage your puppy's teeth.

Flea spray and tweezers are helpful in case of external parasites. Flea

A muzzle may be legally required in areas where there is a rabies outbreak.

sprays include aerosols, pump-on liquids, and alcohol-based liquids that you can rub on. Flea powders and collars are also available. You will need tweezers to remove ticks.

Golden retriever owners seldom need muzzles for their dogs. However, you should keep one easily accessible, should the need arise. Some foreign countries require all dogs to wear muzzles, so if you are planning such a trip with your golden, you may need one. A muzzle is also a good precaution if your dog is hurt and you must bring it to a veterinarian. A dog in severe pain may react unpredictably, so be prepared. When buying a muzzle, be sure you get one that can be adjusted for size. Remember that there is a big difference between the head of a golden puppy and that of an adult.

Dog Toys

Toys are essential to a dog's well-being. They signify play to a dog, and they let it know that life comprises more than training sessions, eating, and sleeping. Playing with toys gives a dog exercise. In addition, they allow a puppy to develop its survival instincts, as it will attempt to stalk and capture its toys. Giving your puppy toys will also spare your furniture and clothing from teethmarks.

Rawhide bones are excellent for strengthening a golden's teeth and jaw muscles. A puppy's teeth can quickly chew tough rawhide. Therefore, make sure to replace the bone before it becomes small enough for your puppy to swallow it whole. Avoid toys your puppy can shred and swallow, for they can cause choking or a blockage in the stomach.

When choosing toys, make sure they are designed for dogs and are made of non-toxic materials. Some forms of plastic are toxic, and many forms of wood splinter. In addition, be careful with painted items. Some older types of paint contain lead, which if swallowed in excess can be poisonous and even fatal. To be safe, avoid all painted or varnished toys.

A golden puppy will chew almost anything that will fit into its mouth. It will also tend to seek out anything with

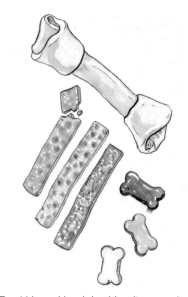

Rawhide and hard dog biscuits come in a wide variety of shapes and sizes. As a golden will most likely make quick work of these, be sure they are of an adequate size to occupy your dog for a sufficient amount of time.

There are several toys available at your pet retailer, such as this tugging rope and pull ring, which help strengthen and clean your dog's teeth and gums.

your scent, such as your old shoes and clothing. For this reason, keep these items out of your puppy's reach. Also, never give your puppy either your old slippers or toys that resemble valuable objects. To a golden puppy, there is little difference between a toy slipper and a real one. This is true of anything of value to you: letters, money, keys, baseball gloves, and so on. Keep all valuable items away from your puppy, and you will prevent the development of bad habits.

My tip: If you are looking for toys around your house, I recommend cardboard boxes, shopping bags, and large balls such as tennis balls. (Golf balls, ping pong balls and the like should *not* be used because they can be chewed apart and swallowed.) These simple household objects can entertain a puppy for hours.

Caring for a Golden Retriever

Before the Puppy Comes Home

Take a few steps now to reduce the confusion when you bring your puppy home. In addition to purchasing necessary equipment and accessories, you should also choose the puppy's food and purchase a supply of it.

When you have bought all the supplies and have placed them in readily accessible locations, begin to "puppy-proof" your home. Remember that a young puppy is very curious, and as it roams through your house it will sniff, paw at, and chew almost everything. For this reason, place all potential hazards out of the puppy's reach.

Remove all poisons, including paints, cleaners, disinfectants, insecticides, and antifreeze. Store them in an area your puppy will have absolutely no access to. Also, remove all sharp objects such as broken glass, nails, and staples. If you have an older home, make sure your dog does not eat paint chips containing lead.

Electrical wires must also be moved out of your puppy's reach. A dog chewing on electrical wires can be injured or killed by the resulting shock.

Rules of Puppy Safety

Before you bring your puppy home review the following seven rules with your family and friends. In addition to preventing injury to the puppy, these rules will help your new pet to feel comfortable and safe in your home.

1. Avoid unnecessary excitement. New owners have a tendency to invite over everyone they know to see their puppy, and young visitors will usually run around, screaming with glee. Let the puppy adjust to its new surroundings before you subject it to numerous strangers.

2. Be sure that everyone in your household knows the proper way to lift and carry the puppy (see page 23). If any visitors express a desire to pick up the puppy, instruct them how to do so.

3. Avoid picking up the puppy too much. Allow it to do its own walking as much as possible, so that it will get needed exercise and added confidence in its own physical abilities.

4. Prohibit rough play. Puppies are fragile creatures and should be handled with care until they grow larger and more mature. Therefore you should avoid overhandling, and make sure that children do not prod or poke the puppy, probe into its ears, or subject it to any other rough handling.

5. Do not subject your puppy to unnecessary heights. Avoid placing it on tables, counters, or beds, because a fall could be disastrous. When it is necessary to place the puppy on an elevated surface, as when you are examining or grooming it, someone must be present the entire time to ensure the puppy's safety.

6. Do not give bones or other very hard objects to a young puppy. Until the puppy reaches about six months of age, it has only its milk teeth and cannot chew hard objects such as meat bones.

7. Try never to leave the puppy unsupervised during the first few weeks.

curtains). Once it spots a target, the puppy will attempt to render it helpless. It will use teeth, paws, and if necessary, all its body weight to accomplish this feat. Hopefully, you will return before the puppy decides to mark off its territory.

Soon after your puppy arrives, you must begin to train it. Training will require time, energy, patience, understanding, and of course, love. From the minute your golden arrives, begin to teach it its name. Other essential lessons are described in detail in the chapter, "Basic and Advanced Training." Remember, the longer you wait to begin training, the harder it will be for your dog to learn.

Lifting and Carrying a Golden Retriever

It is very important for everyone in your family to learn how to lift and carry your puppy. Improper handling can cause pain and even injury. Place one hand under the puppy's chest and support the rear and hind legs with the

A boy and his golden enjoy one last loving moment together before bedtime.

other hand. Never pick up the puppy by placing only one hand under its abdomen, and never pick it up by the scruff of the neck. Both of these methods can hurt the puppy.

You should carry an adult golden only if it is injured or sick. When moving an injured dog, take special precautions. If possible, wait for an experienced person to lift and carry the dog. If you must do this yourself, first place a muzzle on the dog, for a dog in pain may act unpredictably and snap at anyone who tries to help it. Place both of your arms between the dog's four legs and lift. Do not allow the dog's midsection to sag or its head to fall forward. If the dog's weight and size are too great for you, lay it on its side on a blanket or stretcher, and carry it with the help of another person. For further information on treating an injured dog, consult the chapter, "Ailments and Illnesses."

Golden Retrievers and Children

One of the greatest pleasures of owning a golden retriever is watching it play with children. A mature golden seems to know instinctively that children are more fragile than adults, and it will be more gentle when playing with youngsters. Younger and more excitable goldens may have trouble controlling their natural exuberance when playing with children. A golden

The proper way to lift and carry your puppy. Support the puppy's rear and hind legs with one hand, and hold its chest with the other.

There is nothing as natural in this world as a golden retriever puppy at play with a child.

puppy plays rambunctiously both with its littermates and with children. Therefore, when a young dog plays with children, it should always be supervised.

A special bond forms between a golden and children. Golden retrievers tolerate tremendous pushing, pulling, pinching, and ear and tail tugging from boisterous children. In fact, they seem to enjoy the attention more than they mind the pain. The golden's coat and skin are extremely tough, for a hunting dog must be able to cope with all types of weather and to run through dense woods and thickets.

However, because the golden does have vulnerable areas such as its eyes and nose, teach your children the proper way to handle their pet. Children should be taught to never disturb a golden while it is eating or sleeping. Explain that although the dog is a loving pet, it may nip at them if surprised or frightened. Also teach your children how to meet a strange

dog. They should not go to the dog, but let it approach them. They should not move suddenly, and they should keep their hands below the dog's head. If the dog sniffs their hands, and is still friendly, it is all right to pet it.

You can help assure an enduring relationship between your children and your golden by involving them in the responsibilities of dog care. Encourage your children to help feed, groom, and walk your dog.

The Golden and the New Baby

Reports of attacks on infants by family dogs lead many people to get rid of their devoted pets when they have a new baby. This is truly a shame, for goldens are at their best when they have children—including infants—to love. If you have or are planning to have a baby, take heart. Animal behavior experts who have studied this problem thoroughly have concluded that most dogs will not be aggressive toward a baby. They also

As a child and golden grow up together, a special bond will form that will have a lasting beneficial effect on both of them.

believe, however, that dogs that tend to chase and kill small animals, or those that are aggressive toward people in general, should never be left unsupervised with an infant.

You should take several precautions to make sure your golden will readily accept your new baby. Train your dog to sit or lie down for long periods of time before the baby is born. As you increase the length of time the dog remains still, accustom it to other activities occurring around it at the same time. Reward your dog if it stays still and does not attempt to follow you.

Once training is complete, simulate the other activities that will occur after the baby arrives. Use a doll to imitate carrying, feeding, changing, and bathing the newborn.

After the birth of the infant, give the dog something the baby used in the hospital in order for it to sniff and become accustomed to the baby's scent. Upon returning home from the hospital, allow the mother to greet the dog without the baby. Then place the baby in the nursery and deny the dog access by using a screen door or folding gate. In this way the dog can see and hear the infant and get used to its presence before they actually meet.

When you finally introduce dog and baby, one person should control and reward the dog while another person holds the baby. Have the dog sit and then show it to the baby. Keep them together for as long as the dog remains calm. For the next week or two, gradually increase the length of the dog's visit.

Never allow your dog to wander unsupervised in the presence of an infant. However, be sure to include your dog in all the activities that involve your newborn. Do not let the dog feel neglected because of the infant. The more activities in which you allow the dog to participate, the stronger the bond will be between golden and child.

25

HOW-TO:
Grooming a Golden Retriever

Grooming your golden retriever is a simple task that should take no more than about a half hour. You should groom the dog at least once every two weeks.

Equipment

In order to keep your golden in top condition you will need the following equipment: pin brush, slicker brush, comb, scissors or electric clipper, nail clippers, styptic powder, toothbrush, and canine toothpaste (available from your veterinarian).

Having the right equipment is an important part of grooming your golden. Combs, brushes, scissors, and nail clippers are all needed to groom your dog properly, while electric clippers can make parts of the process much easier.

Professional groomers may use a wider variety of equipment such as wide and narrow tooth combs, bristle brushes, or a stripping knife. However, for the purpose of routine grooming, these extra tools may not be needed.

Coat Care

Start by giving your dog a thorough brushing. Use a slicker brush on the major portions of the body. Gently untangle any matted hair or knots with the slicker brush, being careful not to pull out the hair or cause the dog pain by brushing too vigorously. Then brush the coat again using a pin brush. You should feel no tangles as you brush through the coat. Also use the pin brush for the feathering on the legs, chest, and tail. After brushing, comb the entire coat to remove any loose hairs that the brushing may have missed.

While brushing, look for signs of external parasites such as fleas and ticks. If you see any, spray or powder the dog immediately. These parasites may be harder to eliminate if you leave them to multiply. If you note any unusual skin conditions, contact your veterinarian for advice.

Some goldens grow a great deal of soft hair on or around their ears, which may be trimmed to improve their appearance. In addition, you can trim any long or straggly hair growing around the edge of the ears. You should also trim the hair between the pads of your dog's feet. Cut this hair as short as possible. This will reduce the chance of infection in damp weather, and will also improve the dog's traction. Trim the dog's feathering if it becomes excessively long.

Bathing

The golden retriever is a double-coated breed. Excessive bathing will promote the shedding of the undercoat, so bathe your dog only when necessary. If the dog's underside or legs are dirty, wash them with a wet, soapy cloth.

When a bath is necessary, purchase a high-quality dog shampoo. After shampooing, be sure to rinse out the shampoo thoroughly. Soap that is not rinsed out may irritate your dog's skin. If you wish, use a cream rinse to give the coat more body and make the hair easier to comb. Then towel the dog dry. Rub the dog briskly with a large towel in order to remove most of the water. Then brush and comb its coat. Keep the dog indoors and away from drafts while it is drying.

Trimming the Nails

If your dog is active and gets plenty of exercise, you will not need to trim its nails regularly. However, nails can grow back quickly on a "house dog," which may require frequent trimming. Before you trim your dog's nails, be sure you learn how to use a pair of clippers. Improper use of nail clippers can cause your dog a great deal of pain. An experienced dog groomer or a veterinarian can show you how to use them. The center of a dog's nail (called the "quick") contains a blood vessel and nerve endings. You can see these when you examine the dog's claws. If you cut the quick, your dog will suffer much pain.

Clipping nails. Several types of clippers are available. The guillotine-type, shown here, works well.

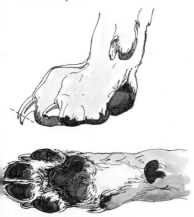

Clip your golden's nail at an angle, making sure not to cut the "quick."

The quick grows out as your dog's nail lengthens. If you wait too long between pedicures, you may have to cut the quick in order to clip the nail back to a comfortable length. Always clip the nail as close to the quick as possible, and be sure to hold the dog's paws firmly but gently. If you accidentally cut the nail too short, it will bleed. Stop the bleeding by using styptic powder.

Tooth Care

Proper tooth care begins with feeding your golden plenty of hard foods, such as dog biscuits and rawhide bones, to help prevent the buildup of tartar. Excessive tartar can lead to deterioration of the gums and tooth loss. Brush your dog's teeth once a week with a toothbrush, using baking soda or preferably a special canine toothpaste. Before brushing, check the dog's teeth and gums for signs of infection or tartar buildup. Excessive tartar buildup will have to be scraped off by your veterinarian.

Ear and Eye Care

As part of your daily grooming routine, be sure to check that

Check on the condition of your golden's teeth and gums at least once a week.

your dog's ears are free of wax and dirt, and its eyes are clear and free of discharge. You can clean around your dog's eyes using a moistened cotton ball to remove any dirt. Use a fresh cotton ball for each eye. If you notice any discharge or inflammation, consult your veterinarian for advice. To clean your golden's ear, hold it open with one hand and gently clean the inside of the flap with a small piece of moistened cotton. Again use a fresh piece for each ear. Be careful not to probe too deeply into the ear canal.

Caution: Before cleaning your dog's eyes and ears for the first time, I recommend that you consult with your veterinarian for the proper way to clean and care for them. An inexperienced owner can cause serious harm to a dog by probing around its ears and eyes. Once you have learned the proper procedures, you will be able to care for these sensitive organs with confidence.

Goldens and Other Pets

Goldens get along very well with all other pets. Your golden will rarely show signs of jealousy as long as it receives sufficient attention. If there is a substantial size difference, such as with birds, hamsters, gerbils, and so on, it is best not to allow these animals to play freely with your golden.

If you own two goldens, you will rarely have any problems; in fact, the dogs will probably enjoy each other's companionship. You must remember, however, not to give the older dog any less attention than previously. If you show the older dog that you care for it as much as always, you may leave the two to establish their own relationship. You should have very little difficulty getting the two dogs to live together in harmony. In fact, if you show no favoritism to either dog, the older one should adopt and protect the younger one.

The Social Behavior of Dogs

If you plan to own more than one golden, or if you wish to understand why dogs react as they do to humans and to each other, you must examine the dog's instinctive nature.

Canine social behavior is very similar to that of wild wolves. Wolves are pack hunting animals and require companionship. This is also true for goldens, though humans can thoroughly satisfy their need for company. Because of this need, you can punish a dog by isolating it during training sessions. In addition, as pack animals, dogs develop among themselves a dominant-subordinate relationship. This relationship allows a stable existence between dogs. Thus, if one of your dogs tends to be more dominant than another, do not worry. This occurs naturally and will prevent fights from breaking out between dogs when competitive situations arise relating to food,

Goldens will usually get along well with all other pets including cats (provided of course, that the other pet is friendly as well).

living space, and human attention. This social ranking is largely determined by size, age, strength, and sex. This social dominance also allows a dog to obey its master, for during training a dog learns that it is subordinate to the human members of the household.

Both dogs and wolves "mark" their frequently traveled paths or territory by urinating, defecating, and scratching the ground. In addition to such boundary marking, females secrete a scent that signals their being in heat.

Social Considerations for a Female Dog

If you own a female golden, you must take special precautions regarding pregnancy. A golden female normally comes into estrus ("in heat" or "in season") twice a year. Estrus is the period during which the female accepts mating with the male. This period usually lasts 9 to 12 days. If you choose to breed your female, refer to the chapter on breeding and the next section. If you choose not to breed your female, you can take sev-

eral measures to prevent pregnancy. As stated earlier, if you plan never to breed the female, have her neutered.

The most obvious way to prevent pregnancy, but probably the hardest, is simply to keep your female away from all male dogs. This can be difficult, however, because male dogs will travel a great distance to find a female in heat. During this time, never let your female outside alone, not even in a fenced-in yard. In addition, during this time always walk your female on a leash. The mating urge between the sexes is very great at this time, and the female may be less obedient and not heed your pleas for her to come back.

Many owners who wish to show their females when they are in heat have their veterinarians administer an estrus control medication. This drug, however, may have side effects. Your veterinarian may also administer chlorophyll tablets to help neutralize the odor of the female's secretions.

When a female is in heat, a bloody discharge may spot your floors and rugs. If your children ask about the

Over the years it has become more and more common to see the multiple golden family, a tribute to just how strongly golden owners feel about their dogs.

bleeding, assure them that it is entirely natural. To prevent staining of your rugs or furniture, you may want to confine your female to an easy-to-clean room. Sanitary napkins and diapers are available for dogs in heat.

Vacationing with Your Golden Retriever

What should you do if you are suddenly called away from home, or if you have planned a vacation and have no family, friends, or neighbors to care for your dog? If you choose not to bring your dog, contact the breeder from whom you purchased it. He or she may be willing to care for it while you are away. If this is not possible, you may wish to place the dog in a boarding kennel. If you plan to do this, be sure to carefully inspect the kennel before leaving your dog there. As previously mentioned, golden retrievers are people-oriented, and many kennels cannot provide the social contact they need. If the kennel can provide the human contact and if the facilities are clean and well managed, a mature golden should have little problem adjusting. You should never leave a puppy younger than six months old at a boarding kennel if you can avoid it.

Of course, you can also take your dog with you. Although this may require some planning and hard work, it can be done. If you plan to travel by air anywhere in the United States or abroad, you'll be glad to know that all major airlines accept dogs. The airline will supply a large crate and will transport your dog in the pressurized cabins of the luggage compartment. Check the cost and any rules concerning pet transport ahead of time.

All major railroads transport dogs throughout the United States. Most will transport large dogs only if they travel in a shipping crate in the baggage car. Check with the railroad to see whether or not they supply the crate.

When traveling by car, your dog may ride either in its cage or in the back seat. Open the window enough to give it some fresh air, but do not expose it to a draft. Drafts can cause eye, ear, and throat problems. Make rest stops at least every two hours and allow your dog to walk and relieve itself. Keep it on a leash so that it will not run away. The inside of a car can get very hot, so allow your dog to drink regularly. Keep a bottle of water on the floor so it remains cool.

Many young dogs become carsick if they are not used to traveling. To prevent this, obtain tablets for motion sickness from your veterinarian.

If you are traveling abroad, obtain a copy of the country's laws pertaining to dogs. Visit or write the consulate of the country you plan to visit, and request a copy. Most countries have minimal requirements concerning dogs; however, some do have special quarantine regulations. You must also be aware of regulations concerning vaccinations, and you will need a valid health certificate from a licensed veterinarian. In addition, you will need a current certificate of vaccination against rabies (not more than six months old). If you need a veterinarian while traveling abroad, you can get a list from the American Consulate or Embassy in the country you are visiting.

My Tip: When you pack your golden's suitcase for a vacation, remember the following: water dishes, leash, collar, muzzle, blanket (and cage) and brush. If possible, bring enough canned or dry food for the entire trip. Feed your dog only what it is accustomed to, and you should minimize the occurrence of digestive disorders.

Proper Nutrition

Understanding Nutrition

All foods are composed of one or several nutrient groups—proteins, fats, carbohydrates, vitamins, minerals, trace elements, and water. These nutrients are essential for the proper growth and metabolism of a dog. By supplying these nutrients in the correct proportions, you will create a well-balanced diet and insure your dog's proper nutrition.

The type and quantity of nutrients a dog needs depends on several factors. Individual growth rate, the kind of work it does, exercise, metabolism rate, and many environmental factors all influence the quantity of food your dog requires. The amount of food a dog needs changes as it gets older. As a result, a dog may become overweight or underweight if its body requirements have changed but its diet has not. For this reason, you must watch your dog's weight and increase or decrease its food intake when necessary.

The Basic Nutrient Groups

Protein

Protein is one of the most important nutrient groups in your dog's diet. Protein supplies amino acids, which are essential for the growth, development, and maintenance of strong bones and muscles. Proteins also promote the production of infection-battling antibodies and are important in the production of enzymes and hormones. Meat, eggs, fish, milk, and cheese are all excellent sources of protein. In addition, you may add other sources of protein such as wheat germ, soybean meals, and brewers dried yeast to your dog's diet. One of the best meat sources of protein is beef, which you may feed your dog either raw or cooked. Cooking does not greatly change the protein value, but it does reduce the fat content somewhat. On the other hand, cooking does break down many vitamins, rendering them of little nutritional value. To avoid trichinosis, be sure to avoid feeding your dog pork that is not completely cooked. Trichinosis is a condition caused by a parasite that may be found in pigs. This parasite can be destroyed through cooking of the meat.

Chicken is a good source of easily digestible protein. Because it takes less energy to digest chicken meat, it is especially good for weak dogs or those recovering from illnesses. When preparing chicken, remove all bones. Chicken bones are soft and tend to splinter when a dog chews them. These splinters can seriously damage a dog's mouth, throat, and digestive tract.

A dog's diet deficient in protein or a specific amino acid may cause poor growth, weight loss, decreased appetite, blood formation problems and edema, and decreased milk production. Protein deficiencies may also result in poor hair and coat condition, and a reduction in antibodies, which can make a dog more susceptible to numerous diseases.

Fat

Fat is a source of energy and heat, and supplies essential fatty acids to a dog's diet. In addition, fat is the primary carrier of fat-soluble vitamins

Commercial dog food comes in a variety of forms. Be sure that the foods you use are of a high nutritional quality.

A golden's second
best friend is its food
dish. Be sure not to
disturb your dog
while it is eating as
this would cause
digestive upsets.

(A, D, E, and K) and has been shown
to make food more palatable for dogs.
Fat is also necessary for proper skin
and coat development. Fat deficiency
usually results in the hair becoming
coarse and dry and the appearance of
skin lesions. However, the fat found in
meat is usually sufficient to meet a
dog's needs.

Carbohydrates

Carbohydrates include starches and
sugars. They help regulate your gold-
en's energy balance. If a golden's diet
lacks carbohydrates, its body will con-
vert proteins normally used for growth
into needed sugars. Carbohydrates
also supply fiber, which may be
digested to supply energy or may help
prevent diarrhea by absorbing water
in the intestines. Fiber also helps
prevent constipation and other intestinal problems.

Vitamins

Vitamins are extremely important in
preventing numerous illnesses and diseases and in regulating many bodily
functions such as growth and fertility.
Your veterinarian will prescribe the vita-

mins to add to your dog's diet. An
excess of some vitamins may be just
as harmful as a deficiency of them.
Some good sources of vitamins include
brewers yeast, cod liver and wheat
germ oils, fresh greens, carrots, and
fruits. Many vitamins are unstable and
can be destroyed by heat or rancidity.
Therefore, serve only fresh, uncooked
foods as vitamin supplements.

Minerals

Minerals, like vitamins, aid many
body functions. In addition, they help
maintain the acid-base balance within
a dog's body. The two minerals dogs
need most are calcium and phospho-
rous. These minerals, in conjunction
with vitamin D, help develop strong
teeth and bones in puppies and young
dogs. Phosphorus is available in
ample amounts in meats, cereals,
grains, vegetables, and fruits. Many
foods, on the other hand, may not
contain sufficient amounts of calcium
to meet the nutritional requirements of
your golden. Additional calcium can be
supplied to your dog by giving it soft
ribs or calf bones to chew on. Calcium
phosphate tablets are also available,
however, your veterinarian should
establish the dosage because too
much can be as harmful as too little.

Salt, another mineral source, is necessary to maintain a proper water balance.

Trace Elements

Trace elements (including cobalt,
copper, iodine, iron, manganese, sele-
nium, and zinc) are so named
because they are needed only in small
quantities. Enough of these elements
is found in most foods to meet the
needs of a golden retriever.

Water

Water is the most important nutrient
because it is vital to all living cells. The
body of an adult golden contains nearly
60% water. Because a dog's body does

not store much water, an inadequate supply can quickly cause problems and even death. A dog's water intake depends on such factors as air temperature, type of food, amount of exercise, and temperament. Your dog should have water available at all times, or at least three times a day. Never give your dog a great deal of cold water after a strenuous exercise period, for this can cause water intoxication.

Commercial Dog Foods

Three types of commercial dog food are available: dry, semimoist, and canned. Commercial food offers an easy alternative to preparing your dog's meals from scratch. Because dogs are very adaptable, you can choose from many successful commercial formulas, some of which differ greatly in ingredients.

Dry dog foods come in pellets, kibbles, extruded products, or whole biscuits. These foods, as the name suggests, are low in moisture (10 to 12%). They contain mostly grains, cereal by-products, soybean and animal meals, milk products, and fats, as well as vitamin and mineral supplements.

Semimoist dog foods usually contain between 25 and 30% moisture. These foods generally have added preservatives and sugars, that protect against spoilage without refrigeration. They contain many of the same ingredients as the dry type. Semimoist foods are usually shaped like patties or simulated meat chunks.

Canned dog foods are usually very high in moisture (about 75%). One type is nutritionally complete and can be served alone, while the other is a highly palatable food supplement that you can add to dry foods to make them more appealing.

No matter what type of commercial food you choose, be sure to read the label carefully for nutritional information and feeding tips.

Important Note: A complete commercial dog food will provide your golden with balanced amounts of all essential nutrients. These nutrients may be added directly to the formula, or contained in other ingredients that are used.

I strongly urge all dog owners to use a high quality commercial dog food rather than preparing their own. When preparing a dog's food from scratch, it becomes all too easy to give your pet either too much or too little of an essential nutrient. This process is also significantly more expensive and time consuming.

Feeding by Age

Puppies under Five Months Old

Once a puppy is weaned from its mother, it is your responsibility to feed it properly. A puppy requires about twice the nutrients per pound of body weight as an adult dog. Because a puppy grows extremely rapidly, it is important that it get substantial protein, therefore, purchase a high-quality commercial puppy food. A golden puppy may eat the equivalent of 10% of its body weight daily. Feed a puppy younger than five months old three times a day.

Indoors or out, make sure your golden always has plenty of clean fresh water.

Remember to start feeding your puppy the same food and on the same schedule used by the breeder. Any changes in diet should be made gradually. Always serve your puppy's food at room temperature, and always keep a fresh supply of water in your puppy's dish. Make sure the water is not too cold, especially during the winter, for this can give the puppy chills. Also, be sure to thoroughly wash your puppy's food and water dishes every day. Harmful bacteria and fungi can grow quickly in bowls that are not regularly cleaned.

At 14 weeks of age, the puppy's permanent teeth begin to push through the gums, causing pain. To ease the puppy's discomfort, give it a rawhide bone to chew on.

Puppies Five to Seven Months Old

At this age, reduce the feedings to two a day. If your dog becomes too fat or too thin, increase or decrease its food intake accordingly. During this period you will probably continue to increase your puppy's food because it is still growing. Add vitamin and mineral supplements in accordance with your veterinarian's advice.

Puppies Seven to Ten Months Old

During this period your dog will begin to reach maturity and will need less food. Continue to give it two meals daily; however, you may begin to serve smaller helpings. Obtain a commercial diet suitable for older puppies.

Feeding Adult Dogs

Coat condition and physical activity are the best indicators of a properly fed dog. A proper diet produces a smooth, soft, shiny coat with rich color. Improperly fed dogs have dull, coarse coats and appear lethargic and fatigued.

How much you feed your adult golden depends on its weight and activity. An outgoing retriever used in hunting needs a higher energy food and more of it than a golden that gets less exercise. In addition, temperament, age, and sex all have a bearing on how much food the dog requires. The best way to monitor how much food your dog needs is to weigh it every few weeks. If your dog is gaining weight, reduce its food and fat intake, and give it more exercise.

Environment also has a large bearing on a golden's food intake. A dog kept in an outdoor run in cold weather needs more than 50% more calories than it would if kept in a warm environment.

Although an adult dog is no longer growing, its digestive system needs to be in a steady working condition so the dog may maintain a healthy metabolism and absorb nutrients properly. To satisfy this need, decrease the protein in your adult dog's diet and increase the carbohydrates. Add carbohydrates high in fiber.

Important Note: If you give your dog a well-balanced diet, it will thrive on it for its entire life. A dog will not become tired of the "same old thing" if it is not given a variety of foods. If your dog does not eat, something is wrong emotionally or physically. Although I am not implying that giving your dog a variety of foods is bad, I do wish to point out that loss of appetite indicates a problem. It may be no more than a mild stomach upset; however, if your dog falls off its diet for two or three days, take it to your veterinarian.

Take note when your dog's movements or gait become hindered. A scratched paw could be the cause, but only investigation can confirm that nothing more serious is involved.

Observe how your dog acts when it lies down. Restlessness may be a symptom of a larger problem.

Healthy goldens, like those shown here, will appear alert and attentive even at rest.

Preventive Medicine

You can take many preventive measures to keep your dog from becoming ill. Prevention starts with a well-balanced diet. Proper hygiene, an adequate exercise program, and a satisfactory dog-master relationship are also important. Finally, be sure to have your puppy vaccinated against common communicable diseases.

Vaccinations

Dogs are vaccinated to prevent them from contracting infectious diseases. These diseases are usually caused by bacteria or viruses and can spread rapidly throughout the dog population. Vaccinations do not always guarantee permanent protection, and often annual booster shots are necessary. The two types of immunity are known as passive immunity and active immunity.

A puppy receives passive immunity when it begins to feed on immune mother's milk. The puppy receives antibodies from its mother's milk, or colostrum. These antibodies attack many disease-producing organisms, thus protecting the puppy. In active immunization, dead or weakened pathogens are injected into a puppy's body in order to induce it to manufacture its own antibodies. The puppy's body secretes these antibodies whenever it is challenged by disease-causing organisms.

A reputable breeder has his or her puppies vaccinated before selling them, and should supply you with a record of this. It takes three or four weeks for an immunization to become fully effective. Your veterinarian should keep a record of all your dog's immunizations. (You will need this record it you plan to travel abroad with your dog).

Preventing Infectious Diseases

Canine Distemper: With the exception of rabies, canine distemper was once the most dangerous known dog disease. A highly contagious virus, it is spread through the urine, feces, saliva, and nasal discharge of the infected animal. The virus may also be carried on blankets, brushes, and clothing. Now, however, dogs vaccinated against distemper will not contract the disease easily.

If the puppy's mother was properly vaccinated against distemper, she is able to passively immunize her newborn puppies. Such immunization lasts through nursing. After weaning, the puppies will need additional vaccinations. Bear in mind that canine distemper is very dangerous and can be very difficult to treat. Thus, vaccinating your dog is extremely important.

Early symptoms of distemper include high fever, diarrhea, dry cough, depression, and mucus-laden discharge from the eyes and nose. Advanced symptoms may include cramps, loss of equilibrium, twitching of leg and facial muscles, partial paralysis, and convulsive seizures. Vaccinations and booster shots are the only effective protection against this disease. Canine distemper is almost always fatal to a young dog that has not been immunized. In older dogs the disease often causes nerve damage.

Canine Hepatitis: This disease should not be confused with human hepatitis. Canine hepatitis is caused by a virus that primarily attacks the liver and gastrointestinal tract. Dogs contract this virus in much the same manner as they do canine distemper. Although humans may carry the virus on their clothing, they cannot catch it. Vaccinated dogs rarely contract this disease. Canine hepatitis is often fatal to an unvaccinated puppy, however. Veterinarians can sometimes save an adult dog.

The symptoms of canine hepatitis include high fever, diarrhea, inflammation of the nasal passages, severe thirst, listlessness, and liver inflamma-

Vaccination against communicable diseases is one of the most important steps in keeping your dog healthy.

tion that makes the abdomen sensitive to the touch. Dogs with canine hepatitis also tend to arch their backs and rub their bellies on the floor in an attempt to relieve the pain in their livers and stomachs. Canine hepatitis develops very rapidly—a dog may appear healthy one day and very ill the next.

Leptospirosis: Leptospirosis is caused by bacteria transmitted through the urine of rats, mice, or an infected dog. Dogs must ingest the bacteria to contract the disease, which attacks the kidneys and liver.

The symptoms of leptospirosis are very similar to those of canine distemper and canine hepatitis; however, leptospirosis usually causes a kidney infection that changes the color and odor of the urine. The urine of an infected dog has a deep yellow to orange color and a strong, offensive odor.

Leptospirosis causes a dog great pain; if not treated in its early stages, it is almost always fatal. On some occasions, leptospirosis has been transmitted to humans. Vaccinations against this disease are the only way to protect your dog, yourself, and your family.

Parainfluenza and Tracheobronchitis: Parainfluenza refers to various viruses of the upper respiratory system. Tracheobronchitis is also known as kennel cough. Both diseases cause inflammation of the trachea and the bronchi, and both are common whenever and wherever dogs congregate. If you plan to board your dog in a kennel or an animal hospital, you should see that it is inoculated against these diseases.

Rabies: Rabies is a viral infection that attacks the nervous system of all warm-blooded animals, including humans. It is usually transmitted through a bite in which the infected saliva of a rabid animal enters the victim's body.

Early symptoms of rabies include behavioral changes. An infected dog may be irritable one minute and friendly the next. Later symptoms include frequent urination and attempts to bite or eat foreign objects such as wood and stones. The dog then becomes vicious, drools excessively, and has difficulty swallowing. Finally, the dog becomes paralyzed, cannot eat or drink, and dies shortly thereafter.

Every dog should be vaccinated against rabies. Because rabies is dangerous to humans as well as dogs, the disease is considered a public health hazard. Any suspicion of rabies should be reported to public health authorities.

Parvovirus: Parvovirus only began to appear in dogs a few years ago. Puppies should be vaccinated before their 14th week. The virus is carried and transmitted in much the same way as is canine distemper.

Two forms of parvovirus are known. One causes an inflammation of the heart muscles of very young puppies. Infected animals quickly collapse and die of heart failure. The more common form, parvoviral enteritis, is characterized by constant vomiting of a foamy, yellow-brown liquid and bloody, foul-smelling diarrhea. Patting the abdomen of an infected dog will cause it to wince in pain. Parvoviral enteritis occurs in dogs of all ages and results in heavy loss of fluids. This leads to severe dehydration and death within a few days.

If the disease is detected early enough, an unvaccinated dog may be saved by intense treatment with intravenous fluids and antibiotics. However, immunization against parvovirus is the best protection.

Vaccination Schedule

Prior to Mating: If you intend to breed your female, bring her to your veterinarian prior to her "season." She can then receive any necessary booster shots and have her stool checked for worms. This will give her puppies passive immunity for about four to six weeks, provided she will nurse them.

Temporary Inoculations: Starting at four to six weeks of age, a puppy's passive immunity begins to wear off. Your veterinarian will then administer a series of temporary injections. Your puppy should receive shots against distemper, canine hepatitis, leptospirosis, parainfluenza, and parvovirus. Then every three or four weeks, until your puppy is four months old, it should receive additional temporary injections.

Annual Booster Shots: By having your dog inoculated every year, you can provide it maximum protection against these infectious diseases.

Of Worms and Worming

Roundworms are by far the most common internal parasites found in dogs. They are white, cylindrical in shape, and can grow up to 4 inches (10 cm). The adult worm embeds itself in the dog's intestinal tract to lay its eggs. The eggs are then passed in the dog's stool. If ingested by another (or the same) animal, the eggs will grow into

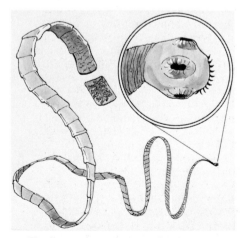

The long, segmented body of the tapeworm. Magnification of the head reveals the hooks and suckers it uses to attach itself to the dog's intestine.

adult worms inside the host and continue the cycle. Although roundworms rarely cause serious illnesses in adult dogs, they can be fatal to a heavily infested puppy. Roundworms are frequently found in newborn puppies if their mother was infected during pregnancy.

Symptoms of roundworm infestation include irregular appetite, diarrhea, weakness, cramps, bloated belly, and in severe cases, paralysis. In addition, the dog's anus may itch, in which case it will skid its rump across the floor in an attempt to scratch it.

Tapeworms infest young and adult dogs and are very tenacious. The head of this worm has hooks and suckers that it uses to attach itself to the dog's small intestines. There it grows into a long chain of segments. The tail segment contains many eggs; occasionally the worm releases the segments, which are passed in the dog's stool.

Symptoms of tapeworm infestation, which are similar to those of roundworm infections, may take a long time to develop. Tapeworms are usually diagnosed by examining the stool. Fleas are the most common source of tapeworms, although your golden may also get other forms from eating infected, uncooked meat (especially beef, pork, and lamb). Your veterinarian will treat tapeworms by destroying the worm's head.

Heartworm disease is very serious and can be fatal if not treated promptly. Heartworms are large worms that attach themselves to the right side of the heart and parts of the lungs. They cause the heart to work harder. As a result, the dog's heart ages rapidly and eventually weakens, thereby affecting all other bodily organs.

Heartworms are transmitted by mosquitoes that carry the worms' larvae. When the mosquito bites a dog, the larvae can enter the dog's bloodstream. It takes about six months for the larvae to develop into mature worms.